Keep ever before you that which you seek;
what is the end to be achieved.

Thomas More

I. WHY EVALUATE?

Many nonprofit boards look forward to a serious assessment of organizational performance in roughly the way a 10-year-old anticipates a dental appointment.

There are many reasons for this. Board members may not want to seem critical of a valued chief executive. They may worry about conflict within the board if the favorite program of an influential member receives poor grades. They may believe that evaluation is properly a responsibility of staff, not board. They may regard evaluation as heartless when the organization depends on devoted persons volunteering their time or accepting lower salaries than they might earn in business. They may fear embarrassment or criticism if the assessment is negative. They may not be sure how to proceed, especially if it is not obvious — and it rarely is obvious — how to measure success. And the right occasion may never quite appear: Board meetings may be infrequent or wholly absorbed in reviews of activities and finances and personnel policies and compensation and considering new programs and reviewing compensation and ... and .... and....

Understandable as those considerations are, no board should lean on them for long. Boards have many jobs to do. (*Ten Basic Responsibilities of Nonprofit Boards*, the first booklet in this series, provides an excellent introduction to them.) But fundamental to them all is the answer to the question: How well is this organization achieving its purposes? Boards are the bridge between an organization and its external environment. Their main jobs are to ensure that the organization is adequately supported by that environment, and that its performance fully justifies that support. And of those two tasks, the second is the more essential because funds that the organization fails to raise remain available for other purposes, but funds it uses poorly, in failed or quixotic or grossly inefficient programs, are simply wasted.

In the commercial world, a continuous flow of data on sales, profitability, and market share make clear whether the business is achieving its purposes. Profit, in particular, tells the corporation that its products or services are selling for more than the costs of the facilities, materials, and labor that it took to produce them. So, crudely but powerfully, profit measures the value society places on having those resources produce those outputs. But no such routinely calculable measure tells a nonprofit, even approximately, whether society values what it produces as much as what it absorbs. Still less is there any automatic indication of whether a nonprofit's resources might be used more effectively. Only periodic evaluations of the organization's work can provide such information. Evaluation is the organization's substitute — and the board's — for the marketplace.

Without such assessments, moreover, boards have no solid basis for performing their other tasks. A board cannot knowledgeably review executive performance, ensure organizational planning, help secure adequate funding, approve and monitor programs, ensure public regard, or assess its own performance unless it knows whether and how well the organization is achieving its purposes.

Finally, there is a defensive reason for serious evaluation. American society accords nonprofits remarkable freedom. They are largely exempt from both taxes and regulation. The implicit bargain is that, in return, they will regulate themselves and provide a public benefit. Boards are society's oversight mechanism. It is up to them to ensure that nonprofits carry out their side of the bargain. If, across the nonprofit sector, they fail to do that, the eventual result will be closer regulation, or the imposition of taxes, or both.

II. EVALUATE WHAT?

Nonprofit boards must oversee many aspects of internal operation: program direction, budget realism, the chief executive's performance, and so on. Each of those responsibilities may benefit, from time to time, from a special assessment or review. But important as they are, such issues share a limitation. They all have to do with processes, inputs, and means. They have to do with how the organization functions. In the end, what counts is something else: output — what the organization achieves. More exactly, it is the relation of inputs to outputs — what the organization achieves in light of the resources it absorbs. The organization does not exist to house a chief executive, however able; or to employ staff, however well-organized; or to stimulate self-examination, however candid; or to ensure its own funding, however meritorious its cause. The organization exists for an end. The most challenging questions the board can ask, and the most important questions for the board to answer, must therefore deal with ends, with what results are being achieved.

So our concern here is with the evaluation of results — the results being achieved by the organization as a whole, or by a program or project so substantial as to justify the board's close attention.

A careful assessment of results must answer three questions.

1. What are the organization's purposes? The first question is fundamental: What is the organization trying to achieve? If the organization has a mission statement, that statement will provide at least a general answer to this question. If no mission statement exists, now is the time to adopt one. If a more specific statement of goals has been adopted, so much the better. There is no way to tell whether an organization is achieving its purposes unless, somewhere, those purposes are clearly stated.

2. How well are those purposes being achieved? Almost certainly, some goals are being met: Some homeless *are* being housed, some minority students *are* receiving an advanced education, some illnesses *are* being treated, the opera *was* enabled to mount a new production, or whatever. But how fully and efficiently are those ends being attained? What is the quality of that housing? What are the costs per person served? How do quality and costs compare with those of like organizations? Questions on this order must be posed and answered before it will be clear how effectively the organization is doing what it does.

But the task is still not complete. Even when good is done, and even when it is done efficiently, it is done at a cost, an opportunity cost. By absorbing resources, the organization or program precludes the doing of other things. And many other things — many alternative programs — might be as fully consistent with the organization's mission as those it currently undertakes.

3. Are there better ways? Is the organization achieving its mission as fully as its resources permit, or might there be better ways of gaining its ends? If the mission is to care for the homeless, for example, the question might be whether housing is in fact the dominant need; whether, over the longer run, job training, sheltered workshops, drug treatment programs, support groups, or some combination of these would better achieve the ultimate goal than investments solely in housing and food.

Board members accustomed to precision may be uncomfortable with the necessarily uncertain nature of answers to questions about ends. But precision is rarely possible in assessing the value of a product that isn't sold. And when the question is "How does that value compare with the worth of what we might be doing instead?" the uncertainties are multiplied, and answers are even more speculative. But a board must accustom itself to two truths: Roughly right answers to important questions are far more valuable than exact answers to lesser ones; and, for the most important questions, roughly right is all one gets.

III. EVALUATE WHEN, AND HOW?

A. When to Evaluate?

To assess the outcomes achieved by an organization (or a major program), to gauge the efficiency with which those results are obtained, and to knowledgeably assess whether another strategy might better serve the same underlying mission — these take time and effort. Yet the conclusions of such an effort are not likely to differ greatly from those of prior assessments unless considerable time has passed, or unless the nature of the organization or program, or of the need it addresses, has substantially changed. It follows that evaluations of this kind need not be undertaken very frequently.

How frequently? No schedule can fit all circumstances, but a reasonable rule of thumb is that such evaluations should be undertaken every three to six years. The more stable the circumstances, the closer to six years; the less stable, the closer to three.

There are two main exceptions to that rule. The first is that, regardless of how stable the circumstances have been, assessment should be undertaken whenever board members or the chief executive have reason to be concerned about the continued utility, efficiency, or effectiveness of the organization or of a major program. The second is that when a program or an entire organization is intended as an experiment, evaluation should begin as soon as results appear.

B. Who Should Evaluate?

The evaluation might be performed internally. If the task looks relatively straightforward, the executive director might assign it to a staff person of independent mind, good judgment and whatever analytic skills or experience the particular evaluation requires. If more complex judgments will need to be made, the better procedure is to assign responsibility to a small group. In that way, a balance of perspectives can be achieved, the extensive work involved in a serious evaluation can be completed sooner, and the useful discipline of viewing the organization from the standpoint not of intentions or inputs, but of outcomes, is experienced by a larger fraction of the staff. In either event, the evaluation should proceed under the active supervision of both the chief executive and at least one board member.

There are advantages to conducting the study internally. Costs are low (though other responsibilities of the evaluators will be slighted) and confidentiality may be more readily preserved. But there are also reasons — and generally stronger ones — for having an outsider or group of outsiders perform the evaluation.

Objectivity is the primary reason. However unconsciously, insiders may be influenced by the knowledge that they are assessing their own performance, or that of colleagues. At minimum, the board cannot be confident this is not the case. Note that a concern for objectivity reflects no lack of faith in staff. It is an old truth that the lawyer who represents his own cause has a fool for a client. Physicians, similarly, do not normally treat their own families. The reason is not incompetence or bias; it is simply that excessive closeness skews judgment.

Skills are a second reason for engaging an outsider. Depending on the subject matter, the evaluation may call not merely for hard work and general good judgment, but also for skill in survey design or quantitative analysis, expertise in some technical field, mastery of relevant literature, or simply experience at evaluation. No insider may be able to provide all of those skills.

A third reason is time. Although the exact extent of the evaluation will depend on the scale and complexity of its subject, all serious evaluations take substantial time and effort. Diverting skilled staff from their normal responsibilities for an extended period may put an intolerable burden on others.

If the evaluation will not require great effort or high technical skill, it may be possible to find an outsider, or small group of outsiders, willing to perform it on a *pro bono* basis. Such evaluators might be drawn, for example, from the staffs of other nonprofits, from a national organization of which the nonprofit is a member, from local business executives who have served on the boards of effective nonprofits, or thoughtful practitioners in the organization's field. Where needs are more demanding, however, an experienced professional should be selected. The names of suitable candidates can be obtained from board or staff members of sister organizations.

C. What Is the Standard?

If the organization as a whole is being evaluated, the only standard against which to measure its performance may be its mission statement. The more specific the standard the better. If the organization has adopted a statement of goals, set specific objectives as part of a strategic plan, or developed any other measure of what it intends to achieve, the evaluation should assess performance against the most detailed and explicit of those statements.

Evaluation can also shed light on both organizational structure and program effectiveness. For example, evaluation can focus on how a program might be fine-tuned—not necessarily changed or discontinued—to strengthen results.

Where the evaluation is more limited in scope, assessing a particular project or program rather than the organization as a whole, a measure more specific than a mission statement is all the more necessary. But it is far more common for organizations to decide on which actions to undertake than to specify the outcomes those actions should achieve, so no useful measure may exist. In such a case, the evaluator should be given the best retrospective estimate of the board or senior staff as to the results intended. The evaluator should feel free to assess the program against other standards as well, but the organization's own statement of intentions is always relevant, even if offered retrospectively.

D. How Should the Evaluation Be Overseen?

No matter how well-chosen the evaluator and how clear the statement of objectives, the evaluation will often prove unsatisfying unless a group of board members, together with the chief executive, approves the design, budget, and schedule of the study at the outset, and monitors its progress thereafter.

One of the board's standing committees might assume that role, but an *ad hoc* committee formed specially for the purpose is generally preferable. The oversight group should specify at the outset the particular questions that the board and chief executive want answered; it should ensure that the evaluators receive whatever access and support they need, and it should review progress reports in the course of the work. The committee may also wish to receive a draft report or to be briefed by the evaluator before a final report is submitted. The purpose of such a review is not to try to affect the evaluator's conclusions. It is to make sure that all questions of interest have been addressed and that the reasoning behind all findings and recommendations is clear. Such a pre-submission review also gives the oversight committee and the chief executive a chance to consider how the full board might best absorb and discuss the evaluation. The committee might decide to schedule a retreat, for example, for that purpose.

E. What Are Some Key Questions?

The particular questions an evaluation should pursue will depend, of course, on the nature and scope of its subject, and on any specific board concerns. But some generic questions are helpful starting points. For example:

- Suppose we were establishing the organization today. Would we choose to do exactly what we are doing now? Would we do those things in the same way we do now? If not, what would it take to change to the preferred pattern?
- Are the priorities implicit in our programs consistent with those expressed in the mission statement? If not, how might the programs be revised to reflect our mission more fully? Alternatively, if the mission statement were to be redrawn to reflect the objectives implicit in our actions, how might it read?
- Of the various institutions (or programs) analogous to ours, which are the best? How are we like them; how are we different? What changes in staffing, facilities, procedures, or modes of operation would it take for us to reach or exceed their level?
- Suppose that operating a truly effective organization (or program) were a crime, and we were indicted. What would our defense be? Put less melodramatically, what are the most powerful arguments that our work is ineffective?
- Who are the persons we want most to serve? How well do they think we are doing? Who are our constituents, and how do they view us?
- What are the circumstances that most affect our work — levels of need, levels of funding, the relevant technologies, the nature of competing institutions, for example — and how are they likely to change over the next three to five years? What are the implications of such changes for the design of the organization (or program), for its mode of operation, for its staffing, for its budget? Should we begin now to adjust to these changes?

F. The Report Is Submitted. What Then?

Few serious evaluations conclude that perfection has been fully achieved. Most assessments — even of quite successful programs or institutions — find that current deficiencies or changing circumstances suggest substantial change. Change may be proposed in the organization's goals, its strategies for achieving them, its personnel, its processes, its organization, or in any combination of these. But the value of an evaluation is not in what it says, of course; it is in the useful change — if any — that follows. If that value is to be gained, the board, along with the chief executive, must decide on the changes required, must communicate those decisions clearly, and must provide whatever backing is needed to bring them about.

IV. USEFUL BY-PRODUCTS

Well-executed evaluations generate at least three important by-products.

Building a base. Practice doesn't make perfect, but it does make for improvement. Even if a first assessment produces only uncertain or speculative conclusions, the experience is likely to stimulate both board and staff to focus more sharply on results, to consider better measures of success, to seek more telling data—perhaps revising a management information system to produce it routinely — and to question more assumptions. Over time, those changes should improve organizational performance. And subsequent evaluations, based on better measures and more relevant data, will reach more authoritative conclusions.

Sharpening the focus of board concerns. The governing boards of many nonprofits tend passively to accede to the policy proposals of staff, or swing to the opposite fault and second-guess the details of management. Sometimes they do both. The fundamental reason is that it is not clear to many board members what their job is. This booklet is grounded in the view that the job of a board is neither administration nor cheerleading but governance, and that the proper governance of a nonprofit is difficult — more difficult, in fact, than corporate governance because the nonprofit is likely to pursue subtler and more complex objectives than a corporation, and no market routinely tells it how its products are valued. Ensuring financial prudence aside, then, the board's chief task is to substitute for the market — to decide for itself whether the organization's resources are being invested as effectively as possible.

A board that sets this task for itself will stay abreast of the organization's programs, through evaluations and otherwise. The evaluation process is also helpful in bringing board members up to speed on current issues and programs. The board will knowledgeably review major substantive proposals, and it will not spend much time reviewing the purchase of office furniture; its eye will be on the strategic issues that are its most crucial and most interesting responsibilities.

Justifying support. Finally, the nonprofit that puts itself through serious evaluation, and heeds the results, will deserve enhanced support and, over time, is likely to obtain it. Nonprofits are proliferating in the United States, and whether they look for funding to governments, foundations, corporations, or individuals, they all compete for support. To sophisticated donors serious self-evaluation is impressive, and donors are becoming increasingly sophisticated. Over time, therefore, the practice of evaluation should not only produce enhanced performance, but help clarify the relative roles of board and staff, and enhance the organization's appeal to funders.

V. CONCLUSION

The reluctance of boards to commission evaluations is understandable. The process may be unsettling, the results unflattering, the costs substantial. But the potential benefits are fundamental: better organizational performance and more effective use of board time and skills. And in the end the task is unavoidable. To ensure that something important is being accomplished, and accomplished efficiently, is the board's most basic responsibility.

It is an increasingly significant responsibility. The reason is that many nonprofits now play crucial roles. Some are huge (the largest employer in the city of Pittsburgh is not one of the major corporations, it is the University of Pittsburgh). Many nonprofits touch the lives of the neediest and least advantaged among us. Some provide badly needed social services. Most are innovators; indeed, over the long term, the nonprofit sector's greatest value arises exactly from its freedom to experiment. In many realms — social, artistic, medical, educational — nonprofits perform much of our country's research and development. But experiments are useless unless one learns how they came out. That is the question evaluation must answer.

Appendix:
An Evaluation Checklist

1. **When to evaluate?** Normally, every three to six years, and early in that period (or even sooner) if circumstances have greatly changed since the last evaluation, or if the chief executive or board members have some reason for concern.

2. **Who should evaluate?** An internal group or person if they can be spared from normal assignments, have the right qualifications, and will be sufficiently objective. Outsiders whenever those qualifications cannot be fully met.

3. **What is the standard?** The terms in which the mission statement, a strategic plan, or a statement of goals (the more specific the better) define what was expected to be achieved. If no such document exists, the board must specify the standard to be met.

4. **Who should oversee the work?** The chief executive, together with a board oversight committee. They should approve the study's design, budget, and schedule; receive progress reports; review a draft report before the evaluation is concluded; and decide how the full board might best receive and discuss the report.

5. **What might be some key questions?** Specifics will vary with whatever is being evaluated, but generic questions are:

If we were starting today, would we do it this way?

Do our actions match our mission statement?

How are we like and unlike the best in our field?

What do our intended beneficiaries think of our performance?

How are the next five years likely to be different?

6. **The report is submitted. What then?** Implementation is the pay-off. It is the responsibility of the board and the chief executive to make it happen.

Suggested Resources

Carver, John. *Boards That Make a Difference: A New Design for Leadership in Nonprofit and Public Organizations.* San Francisco, CA: Jossey-Bass Publishers, 1990, 266 pages.

This excellent general discussion of board functions and disfunctions and board-staff relations contains a brief section (pp. 77-80) on the importance of evaluation and on its proper focus.

Espy, Siri N. *Handbook of Strategic Planning for Nonprofit Organizations.* New York, NY: Praeger, 1986, 131 pages.

A brief, practical and informal guide to strategic planning with a short but useful section (pp. 120-123) on evaluation as a follow-up to strategic planning.

Hall, Holly. "Assessing the Work of Whole Foundation," in *The Chronicle of Philanthropy*, January 14, 1992.

A detailed account of how the Northwest Area Foundation put itself through a particularly comprehensive externally conducted assessment of its work and impact.

Houle, Cyril O. *Governing Boards: Their Nature and Nurture.* San Francisco, CA: Jossey-Bass Publishers, 1989, 225 pages. (Also available from the National Center for Nonprofit Boards)

A wide-ranging discussion of board responsibilities that includes a section (pp. 147-156) on various forms, uses, and procedures for organizational evaluation.

O'Connel, Brian. *Evaluating Results.* Nonprofit Management Series No. 9. Washington, DC: Independent Sector, 1988, 27 pages.

A brief but helpful guide that stresses the distinctive problems of evaluation in the nonprofit as opposed to the commercial setting.

Newman, Harvey, et al. *Self-Evaluation and Planning for Human Service Organizations.* New York, NY: AMACOM, the American Management Association, 1987, 179 pages.

A detailed and practical handbook for guiding an organization through an internally conducted evaluation. Designed for human service organizations but applicable more broadly.

About the Author

Peter Szanton is president of the Washington, D.C.-based Szanton Associates, consultants to nonprofits on strategic planning and organizational assessment. Mr. Szanton is the author of numerous reports and articles, and of books on national service, federal organization, and the relationships between consultants and their clients. A former associate director of the White House's Office of Management and Budget, Mr. Szanton holds BA, MA, and LLB degrees from Harvard. He is a member of the Council on Foreign Relations and serves on the boards of a number of nonprofit organizations, including Youth Service America and the National Academy of Public Administration.